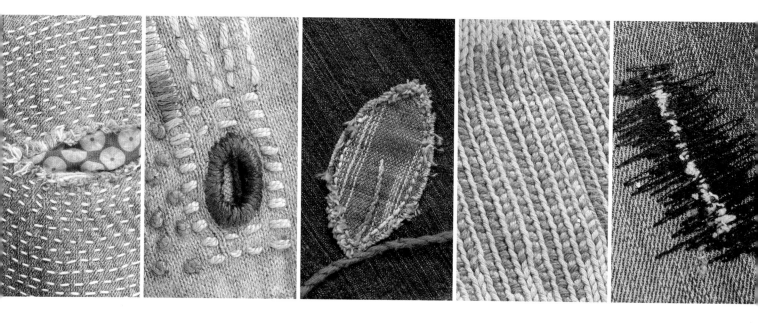

CONTENTS

VISIBLE MENDING

ARTFUL STITCHERY TO REPAIR AND REFRESH YOUR FAVORITE THINGS

Jenny Wilding Cardon

Martingale®
Create with Confidence

Visible Mending: Artful Stitchery to Repair and Refresh Your
Favorite Things
© 2018 by Jenny Wilding Cardon

Martingale®
19021 120th Ave. NE, Ste. 102
Bothell, WA 98011-9511 USA
ShopMartingale.com

Printed in China
23 22 21 20 19 18   8 7 6 5 4 3 2 1

Library of Congress Cataloging-in-Publication Data

Names: Cardon, Jenny Wilding, author.

Title: Visible mending : artful stitchery to repair and refresh your
      favorite things / Jenny Wilding Cardon.

Description: Bothell, WA : Martingale, 2018.

Identifiers: LCCN 2017058191 | ISBN 9781604689358

Subjects: LCSH: Clothing and dress--Repairing. | Needlework.

Classification: LCC TT720 .C37 2018 | DDC 646/.6--dc23

LC record available at https://lccn.loc.gov/2017058191

MISSION STATEMENT

We empower makers who use fabric and yarn
to make life more enjoyable.

CREDITS

**PUBLISHER AND
CHIEF VISIONARY OFFICER**
Jennifer Erbe Keltner

CONTENT DIRECTOR
Karen Costello Soltys

DESIGN MANAGER
Adrienne Smitke

MANAGING EDITOR
Tina Cook

PRODUCTION MANAGER
Regina Girard

ACQUISITIONS EDITOR
Karen M. Burns

PHOTOGRAPHER
Brent Kane

TECHNICAL EDITOR
Amelia Johanson

ILLUSTRATOR
Sandy Loi

COPY EDITOR
Durby Peterson

DEDICATION

*To my dad, George DeWayne Wilding,
who would have been proud.*

VISIBLE MENDING: ART, CRAFT, AND CREATIVITY

Mending a broken heart. Mending fences. Mending your ways. Making amends. On the mend.

Mending is all about making things better, don't you think? We mend family rifts, friendship disagreements, romantic impasses. Sometimes those experiences leave a scar. Perhaps the scars are visible, but they lead to a closer connection and a new kind of beauty. The scars are a testament to our ability to adapt and adjust and alter things for the better.

So why wouldn't we attempt to mend everything in our lives?

"As machines become more and more efficient and perfect, so it will become clear that imperfection is the greatness of man."

–Ernst Fischer

This book comes with an experiment created just for you: to see the beauty in the broken; to get inspired (instead of disappointed) when something "perfect" becomes imperfect; to see every rip, snag, and stain as an opportunity for one-of-a-kind creativity; to appreciate something for what it was, what it's becoming, and what it will be—mends and all.

Visible Mending is half how-to book, half inspiration guide. My goal is to provide a technique book for people who have never sewn before and an inspiration book for people who have been sewing all their lives. With the ideas included, you can finish a mend in minutes or slow down and take your sweet time—the style, the sewing complexity, and the pace at which you complete a mend is entirely up to you.

Follow along, and you'll soon be giving a new life to worn-and-torn items you might otherwise throw away, all while letting your creativity take center stage.

The experiment: Embrace the perfectly imperfect. Make do and mend. Repair it and wear it. Let's get started!

BORO STITCHING

The Japanese people have time-honored philosophies that make a lot of sense to me. There's the tradition of *Wabi-sabi,* an aesthetic that celebrates the imperfect, the impermanent, and the incomplete. *Mottainai* is a term conveying a sense of remorse when something useful goes to waste. (We've all heard the expression "Mottainai!" as the English translation, "What a waste!") *Kintsukuroi* is the art of repairing broken pottery with lacquer, which is dusted with powdered gold, silver, or platinum, literally adding value to something that might otherwise be discarded.

And then there is *boro,* the art of Japanese mending. First used as a necessity by families of farmers and fishermen to reinforce and mend clothing and linens, boro is now regarded as an art form, with galleries staging showings of antique boro-stitched kimonos, blankets, and other fabric items. The examples you can find online are astounding—years upon years of patch upon patch, layer upon layer, stitch upon stitch, all on a single item.

Rather than casting off an item that is blemished or even broken, the Japanese treasure items as being even more beautiful and unique for acquiring flaws and irregularities, eccentricities, and quirks. Because now, that item is a one-of-a-kind item. It has a story and a history. And there is great value in that.

Boro is as life itself is. And because imperfection is an absolute characteristic of boro—meaning, we start with something that is imperfect to begin with—hand stitches (at times wonky and askew and unsteady and uneven) pair flawlessly with the boro style. Whether your stitches are big or small, faultless or flawed, accurate and exact, or carefree and a bit crazy, they'll fit in with the boro aesthetic.

The boro technique gives makers the opportunity to play with improvisation and expression, and it will surprise you with its side perks: meditative therapy—via slow sewing—and the choice to forge an alternate path, away from consumer-driven fast fashion.

That's my contemplation on boro. But in this beginner's introduction to boro stitching, which couldn't be easier to learn, you'll find that the technique is also flat-out fun. Transform any mend (from a stubborn stain to a bit of fraying to a fast-growing hole) into a unique work of art, sewn by you.

"Perfection is boring; let's get weird."

–Emily Henderson, host of HGTV's *Secrets from a Stylist*

MATERIALS FOR BORO STITCHING

For boro you need a mendable item, fabric scraps, scissors, thick thread, and a needle with an eye large enough to pull the thick thread through. If you're shopping for new items to add to your boro bag of tricks, here are a few suggestions.

Item in need of repair. Loose-weave cotton is the fabric typically used for boro-stitched items. But that doesn't mean you can't experiment. As you'll see in the next few pages, you can use the boro technique on light and heavy cottons, denim, and even knit fabric.

Patches. To get the hang of boro stitching, I suggest starting with woven cotton items to mend (think cotton, linen, flannel, denim, and corduroy) and woven cotton patches for the repair, because woven fabric provides the sturdiest foundation for practicing your stitches. Then move on to experimenting with stretchier fabric. For a long-lasting mend, patches should measure at least ½" larger all around than the space to be mended.

Thread. Cotton sashiko thread is great for boro stitching, and you'll find it online in lots of colors. But you can easily substitute cotton embroidery floss, pearl cotton, or even thin yarn. If you use sewing thread, opt for 12-weight or thicker; it will mimic the boro look and is sturdier than common sewing thread.

Embroidery floss is divisible; it comes in six individual strands that can be pulled apart. I like to use all six strands for boro stitching, to get a chunky texture. Sashiko threads, pearl cottons, and yarns aren't divisible—each comes as a single or twisted strand—but pearl cottons and yarns do come in various weights. I prefer size 5 pearl cotton. For yarn, use super fine (size 1). If you prefer to baste with thread rather than glue (I like to baste with both), you'll also need common sewing thread—any kind will do.

> *Double Down*
>
> *Does the thread you're using look too thin, now that you're stitching? Double it. Thread your needle with a length of thread; when you tie a knot at the end, tie both ends together. You'll sew with two strands of thread instead of one, which will give a weightier, chunkier look to your stitches.*

Hand-sewing needles. I use both long and short sashiko needles (Clover's Sashico™ Needles come in a variety of lengths). Chenille needles, which have sharp points and large eyes, also work well. Use long needles when covering large areas with straight running stitches. For smaller areas, use a short needle, especially for curves.

Glue stick. Using a washable glue stick is a quick way to baste your patches and easily reposition them. If you'll be transporting your project as you work on it, I suggest thread basting your patches (page 10) to make sure that they don't shift.

Fabric scissors (necessary); rotary mat, rotary ruler, and rotary cutter (optional). Scissors are a must for cutting patches, snipping thread, and cleaning up loose threads. Rotary-cutting equipment isn't required, but it makes quick work of cutting patches. If you prefer precisely cut shapes to shapes that have a little wonkiness to them, rotary is the way to go.

« Sashiko thread

« 6-strand embroidery floss

« 3-strand embroidery floss

« Pearl cotton, size 5

« 12-weight thread

« Super-fine yarn

Ring thimble (optional). A traditional thimble is helpful for pushing your needle through multiple layers of fabric, but I'm in love with Clover's Adjustable Ring Thimble. You wear it on the middle finger of the hand you sew with—it's like pushing the needle with the palm of your hand. And no sweaty fingertips.

Needle-nose pliers. Sometimes a thimble isn't enough. Try poking through three layers of denim plus an established seam in a garment. Ouch! If you push your needle in but can't get it back out, pliers are great to have on hand. Just make sure your pliers don't have gripper teeth on the blades, which can damage your needle. Look for pliers with smooth blades in the jewelry section of your local craft store.

Marking tools (optional). Washable and air-soluble markers help with planning stitching paths, and they disappear over time or with a little water. For a precise look to your stitches, go with thinner pencils and markers. If you prefer an organic look, skip the marking tools and just start sewing. See page 12 for more about marking designs with pencils and markers in addition to info on printable, wash-away stabilizer.

Thread conditioner (optional). I use a beeswax block to give thread firmness, prevent knotting, and help the thread run smoothly through fabric. To apply, start with a threaded needle. Press on the thread with your finger while running the thread through the beeswax, starting at the needle eye and ending at the thread tail.

Fusible interfacing (optional). Interfacing stabilizes delicate fabric and fabric with stretch. I use the lightest-weight fusible interfacing suitable to the project, and I rarely use interfacing with woven fabric. If you're working with knits, use a lightweight fusible interfacing specifically designed for knit fabric. It's fine to skip interfacing when working with denim—there's already plenty of stability there!

Fusible web (optional). Two-sided fusible web makes it easy to apply scraps and layer patches. Because it adheres on both sides, you can fuse it first to your patch and then fuse the prepared piece to your project (Steam-A-Seam 2 is a brand that's easy to find).

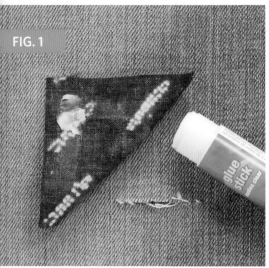

FIG. 1

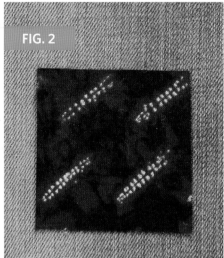

FIG. 2

FIG. 3

Glue basting works well if you're going to sew your patch right away.
Thread basting is great for holding patches in place for longer periods.

Wash-away stabilizer (optional). When sewing large areas or something other than straight stitches, I like to use a guide. I print ¼" graph paper onto sheets of wash-away stabilizer and then thread baste the gridded stabilizer to the project (even though the stabilizer has a sticky back, it doesn't always stay in place). The stabilizer gives me lines to follow, and it's also great for making nearly identical Xs or diagonal lines of stitching. See page 12 for an example. I use Pellon's Stick-N-Washaway. Once you're done stitching, immerse your project in water and give it a swish—the stabilizer easily washes away.

Visit ShopMartingale.com/VisibleMending to print ¼" graph paper for use with wash-away stabilizer sheets.

Cardstock (optional). I use cardstock when I might accidentally stitch through two layers (such as a blown-out knee on a pant leg). I cut the cardstock to match the width of the pant leg and slip it between the pant layers I'm sewing. It stops me from sewing through two layers, thereby avoiding a lot of unpicked stitches (ask me how I know).

LEARNING TO STITCH, BORO STYLE

Boro is so simple to learn—which makes it so much fun! Just a needle, thread, patches, and an item that needs a little TLC are required. There are many ways to get creative, but below are the basic steps. For a video introduction to boro stitching, visit ShopMartingale.com/VisibleMending.

1 Remove any loose threads from the spot to be mended. Glue or thread baste a patch over the area, making sure the patch measures at least ½" larger all around than the mendable area.

To glue baste, dot the wrong side of the patch with a glue stick (fig. 1) and press it onto the area to be mended, making sure to center the patch over the mendable area (fig. 2).

To thread baste, thread a needle with sewing thread, tie a knot at one end, and take large stitches around the edges of the patch. You can also sew an X through the patch to further secure it to the item to be mended (fig. 3). When the patch is secure, tie a knot in the thread close to the surface and cut away any excess thread. To view a quick video on how to tie a quilter's knot, visit ShopMartingale.com/VisibleMending.

2 Thread a long needle with a cut of thread no longer than an arm's length (to avoid tangling, shredding, breaking, and other hassles); knot at one end. Working from the wrong side of your item, bring the needle up ⅛" to ¼" from one corner of the patch. Or start your stitches beyond the patch and work your way toward it, if you like.

3 Sew the patch to the mendable item with a running stitch (fig. 4). Rock your needle back and forth to load more than one stitch onto your needle—this is a time-saver when you're sewing straight lines. You can stitch directly on the patch only or stitch beyond the patch. Take large stitches or small stitches; the look of your stitches is up to you. I've experimented, and I like stitches that are ⅛" to ¼" in length, but it really depends on the project—big stitches look great on some things, and small stitches suit others. Try one stitch length to start, and sew two rows. If you don't like how it looks, take out those rows and start again with a stitch length you prefer.

4 Continue stitching until you've covered the patch (fig. 5). Pull the fabric you've stitched taut every few stitches to avoid puckering or tightening, especially if the part of the garment you're working on will lie against a body part that bends, such as an elbow or knee. You want to keep the fabric flexible in these areas to avoid stress or strain on the stitching.

5 To end your stitching, knot the end of the thread and pull it taut against the wrong side of the project. (Make your knots on the right side of your project if you like that look.) I leave a ½" tail beyond the knot to avoid the thread fraying down to the knot and possibly unraveling.

A hole in a sweatshirt patched with boro stitching (fig. 6). See the completed project on page 18.

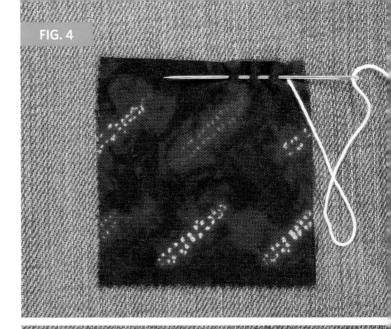

FIG. 4

FIG. 5

FIG. 6

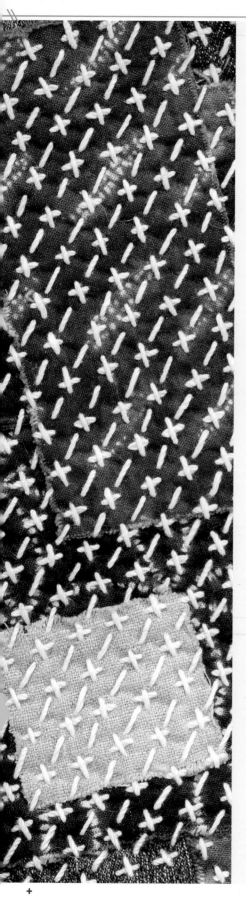

Transferring Stitching Guides

You can sew your stitches freehand or transfer a specific motif to the fabric for your needle to follow. Use chalk, washable or air-soluble markers, or washable colored pencils along with a ruler to draw a uniform pattern. To cover large areas with stitches, or to create a more graphic pattern with your stitches, consider using ¼" graph paper printed onto wash-away stabilizer as shown below.

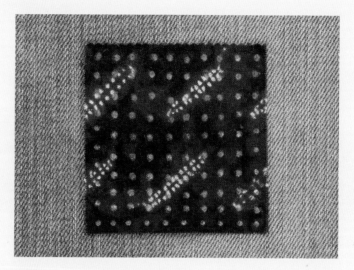

Uniform dots marked with chalk

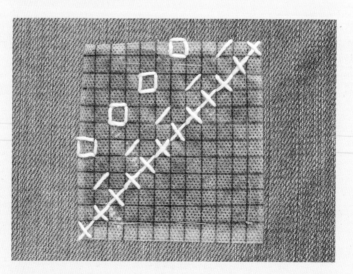

Once you've printed your graph on stabilizer, thread baste the stabilizer over a patch. (I traced the graph paper motif with a ballpoint pen so it could easily be seen for this photo, but you shouldn't have any trouble seeing the lines as you're stitching.)

LAYERING PATCHES FOR STYLE AND STRENGTH

Before you start any stitching—especially if you're trying to mend a large hole—you may want to reinforce the mendable area by adding another patch to the wrong side of the work, or to the right side. Stitch through all layers at the same time.

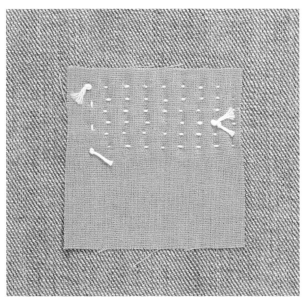 

Add a patch to the back of your work (left) *to reinforce your repair* (right).

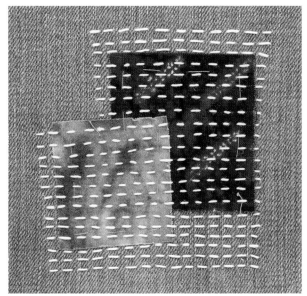 

Left: *Overlap two patches and stitch as a unit.* Right: *Turn a contrasting patch into a design element by cutting it a little larger than the featured patch. Add both patches to the front of your work, with the contrasting patch layered underneath.*

BORO STITCHING GALLERY

Once you get the hang of boro stitching, you can change things up in so many ways!
Here are a few creative examples of different items that are visibly mended with boro.

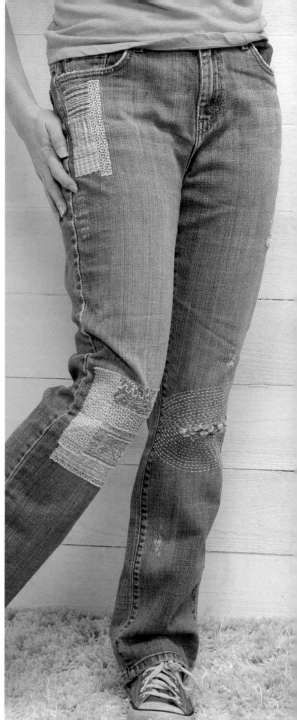

Faded Denim

I used fabric scraps from a coordinated bundle of fabric (available at quilt shops and online) to mend these favorite jeans. I cut fabric strips and squares and layered them where the jeans had holes or where fabric was beginning to wear. On the left knee, I placed the patch underneath the hole instead of on top and then stitched a freehand circular pattern around the hole. On the right leg, I also embroidered the date for each year that I've owned the jeans—since 2012.

Dark Denim

Light blue and indigo cotton patches plus linen patches in ecru cover the wear and tear on these skinny jeans. To create the stitch pattern, I used graph paper printed onto wash-away stabilizer (page 12)—it enabled me to stitch more precise Xs and diagonal stitches. I stitched only within the perimeters on some patches and stitched beyond the patch edge on others—the final look is up to you, so experiment.

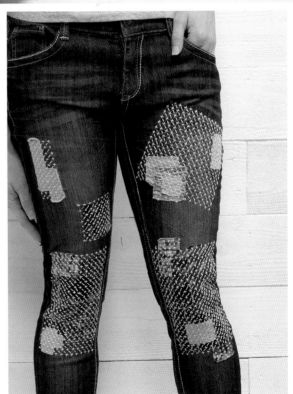

Army Bag

The front flap and heavy canvas strap were in disrepair when I found this army bag at a flea market. I layered fussy-cut cotton prints (a fussy-cut patch is one that's been cut from a specific area of a print; see page 43) and denim patches, and I experimented with a variety of free-form stitches to secure the layers.

For one area of the bag strap, I folded a patch around the edge where the strap was unraveling and secured the patch with straight and diagonal stitches. I didn't like how the back of the patch looked, so I covered it with a strip of canvas that was first secured to the area with double-sided fusible web. Pliers proved invaluable in helping me pull the needle through the heavy strap.

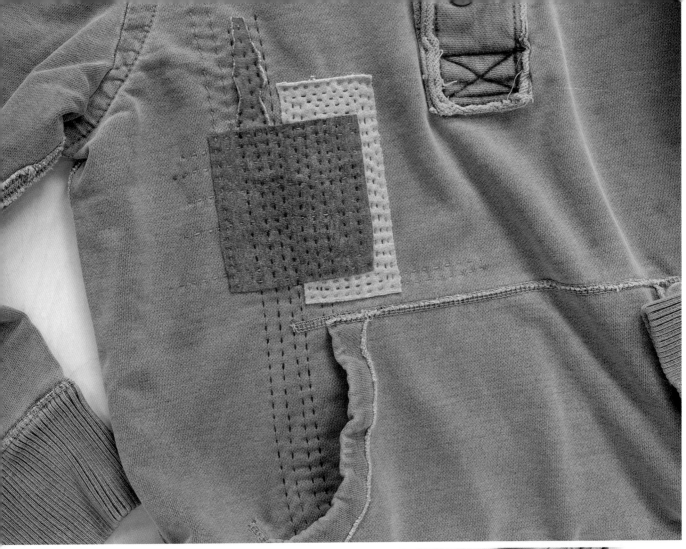

Men's Hoodie

How does my husband inflict such trauma on his clothing? I'll never understand, but it was fun to doctor up his hoodie! I patched the wear and tear with sweatshirt scraps from a previous project, placing patches both on top of and underneath the right side of the garment. I used two thread colors, blue and gray, and let the straight stitches wander.

Black Jacket

A little damage—in this case a hole in the elbow—rarely keeps me from thrifting a cool jacket. To repair my "new" black jacket, I cut arrow/heart shapes (depending on how your eyes see them!) from cotton prints, glue basted and thread basted them to the sleeve, and permanently secured them with horizontal and vertical stitches, using graph paper printed onto wash-away stabilizer as a stitch guide (page 12).

Even though there was nothing wrong with the back of the jacket, I decided to add a similar motif with scraps from the sleeve patches. I ironed random scraps onto fusible web, cut out the motif, and fused it to the back of the jacket. I finished with straight stitches and T stitches (crossed straight stitches), using the graph-paper technique.

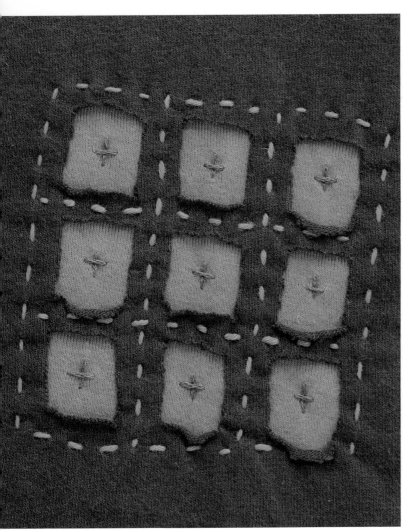

Boy's Knit Shirt

Don't be afraid of knits! I decided to turn a small hole in my 10-year-old's shirt into nine big holes, mimicking the printed checkerboard motif on the shirt. I drew squares on the shirt with an air-soluble marker, snipped into the center of each hole with small, sharp scissors, and then carefully cut out each square. For added stability, I fused a square of teal knit fabric to lightweight fusible web specifically for knit fabric, making sure to cut the teal fabric at least ½" larger all around than the area to mend. After thread basting the teal patch to the wrong side of the shirt, I straight stitched around the squares and then added T stitches to the center of each square. For additional precision, I used a rotary ruler and a water-soluble marker to mark the center of each square before sewing the T stitches.

    When this project was complete, my 10-year-old asked if he could wear it to school the next day. "Sadly, no, Charlie," I explained. "It's for the book now!" He was bummed until I told him to go to his closet and find a different shirt with a hole so we could start a new project together.

Denim Jacket

One of my favorite parts to harvest from denim jeans is the fabric behind the back pockets, because it retains the original color of the denim, while the exposed layer fades. You'll find wonderful color variations when you remove the pockets and the rivets from the back of a pair of jeans!

I dived into my denim scraps to mend this jacket. The holes in the denim patches on the sleeves and one pocket are where I cut out the rivets that hold the pockets in place. I also layered light and dark colorways of a striped cotton print with the denim patches.

HAND EMBROIDERY

Embroidery is a fun technique for visibly mending everything from little holes in a T-shirt to stubborn stains on the Thanksgiving tablecloth. Embroidery can be simple, elaborate, cute, elegant, or playful; it can be followed in a pattern step-by-step or invented with each new stitch. Mending with embroidery can take 10 minutes or an entire weekend, and one project will turn out just as interesting as the next.

You'll find thousands of different embroidery stitches to try—check online or at your local library for books dedicated to the craft. I love to experiment with different stitches, but just a few stitches committed to memory can be combined in endless ways to create extraordinary mends.

In this chapter, you'll learn 10 different embroidery stitches that lend themselves to mending. You'll then see how I combined those stitches in 11 different ways to mend a variety of items. No patches needed!

> *"My soul is fed with needle and thread."*
>
> –Author unknown

MATERIALS FOR EMBROIDERY

Here's what you'll need when embroidering.

Item in need of repair. With embroidery, you can repair a variety of items that are having a mendable moment. Small holes can be quickly mended with needle and thread alone; larger holes may require a backing of stabilizer to make them embroidery friendly. Embroidery is my favorite choice for stains that won't fade. Cover up a blotch by embroidering over it or turn a stain, blemish, or bleach spot into a focal point by embroidering around it.

Embroidery floss or thread. Just like with boro stitching, embroidery floss and pearl cotton are common fibers of choice. Embroidery floss can be delicate or chunky, depending on how many strands of floss you use, and it has a bit of a flat finish. Pearl cotton (I prefer size 5) has more of a raised look and a bit of a sheen. See page 8 for additional information about embroidery floss and pearl cotton. Both are easy to find at your local craft store or online.

Visit ShopMartingale.com/VisibleMending to view my method for pulling strands from embroidery floss.

Avoid a tangled mess! Learn two ways to unwind a skein onto a bobbin when you don't have a friend to help—watch the video at ShopMartingale.com/VisibleMending.

Equipped for Embroidery

A wise woman once said about sewing: it's the art of searching for items you just had two seconds ago. Embroidery requires the use of several small items—do yourself a favor and keep them corralled in one place! A handmade bag, a small makeup bag, or even a plastic zipper-lock bag will do. Then, resolve to always return your supplies to that bag when you're done.

Hand-sewing needles. Inexpensive packs of embroidery needles are easy to find. I love Clover's Gold Eye embroidery needles because they're strong and long-lasting but also because of their trademark golden eye—they're easy to find in a sea of silver eyes! For knit fabric (such as T-shirts), use ballpoint hand-sewing needles or other blunt-tip hand-sewing needles. The blunt tip will push through knit fibers instead of tearing the tiny threads in knit fabric and possibly causing more holes than you started with. A basic rule for needle sizes: choose the thinnest needle that will accommodate the thread you're using.

Wash-away stabilizer or fusible interfacing. To keep embroidered mends sturdy while sewing, I back tiny holes and tears with sticky-back, wash-away stabilizer (temporary). For bigger holes, I back mendable areas with fusible interfacing (permanent). Both types of interfacing are great for providing a reliable foundation on which to stitch. See pages 9 and 10 for additional information about stabilizers and interfacings.

Thimble, thread conditioner, and marking tools (optional). These items will make your embroidery easier and more precise. See page 9 for a detailed explanation of each tool.

LEARNING TO EMBROIDER

Embroidery is all about knowing how to work different stitches. Once you have a few stitches memorized, you can combine, enlarge and reduce, and tweak them to make them your own. If you aren't familiar with the following embroidery stitches, practice each on a piece of fabric that mimics the style of fabric you'll be mending. Once you get the hang of each stitch, try it on a spot to be mended. You can see 10 of my favorite stitches for visible mending on pages 26–28.

Visit ShopMartingale.com/VisibleMending to view a quick video introduction to each embroidery stitch.

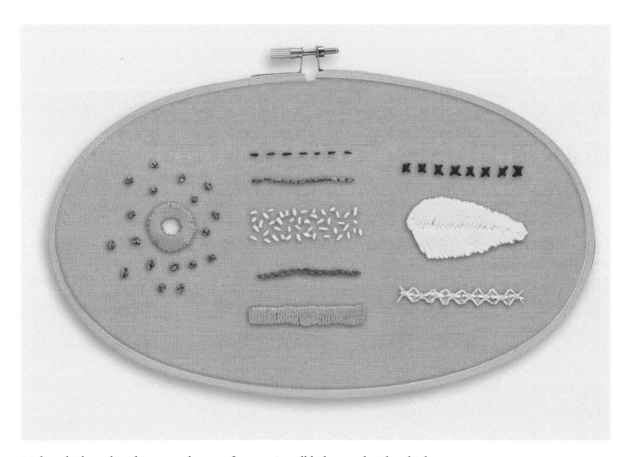

Make a little embroidery sampler to reference; it will help you decide which stitches to use on your project, serve as a reminder of how to work each stitch, and look pretty too! Frame it and hang it in your sewing space for reference.

RUNNING STITCH

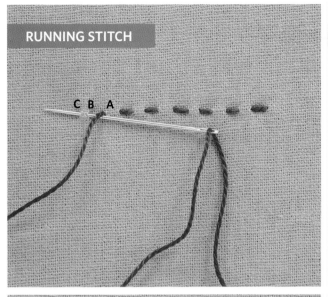

BACKSTITCH

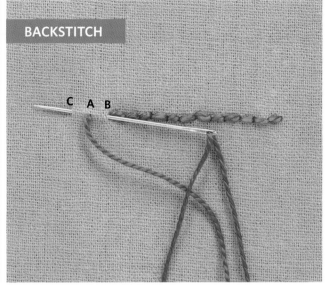

SEED STITCH

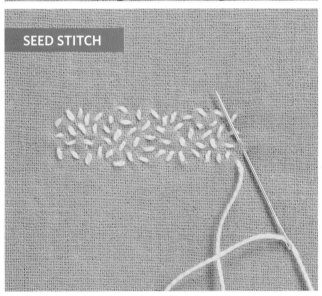

STEM STITCH

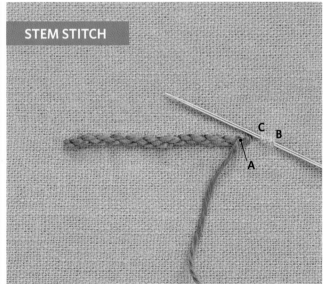

SATIN STITCH

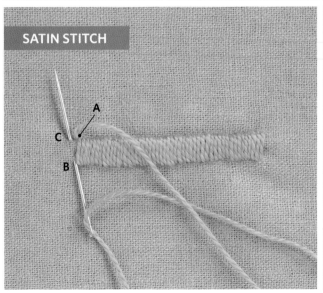

CROSS-STITCH

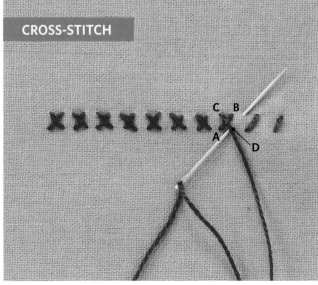

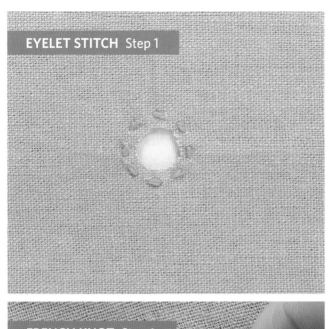

EYELET STITCH Step 1

EYELET STITCH Step 2

FRENCH KNOT Step 1

FRENCH KNOT Step 2

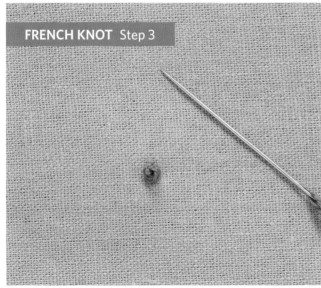

FRENCH KNOT Step 3

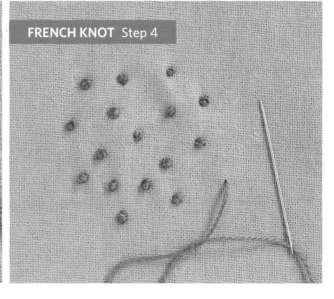

FRENCH KNOT Step 4

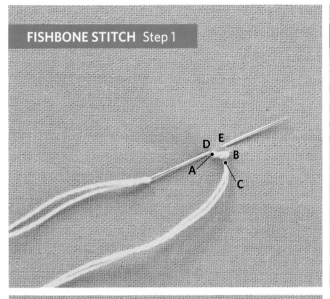

FISHBONE STITCH Step 1

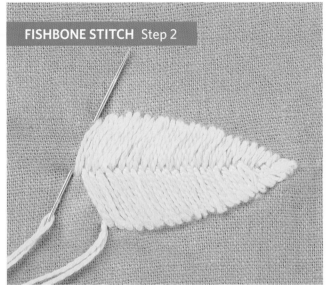

FISHBONE STITCH Step 2

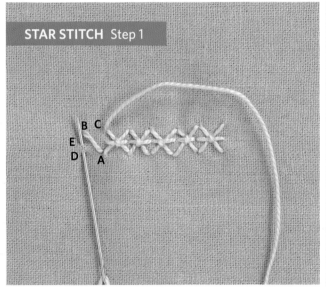

STAR STITCH Step 1

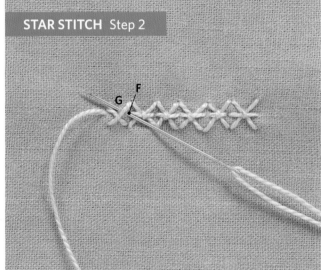

STAR STITCH Step 2

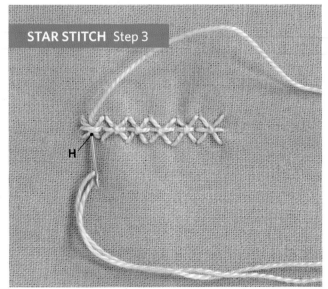

STAR STITCH Step 3

EMBROIDERY GALLERY

Embroidery stitches are easy to learn, and once you've learned the stitches introduced in this book, you'll be armed with the skills to visibly mend items in lots of creative ways (emphasis on creative). I've selected a few of my favorite examples to demonstrate how I've mended with embroidery.

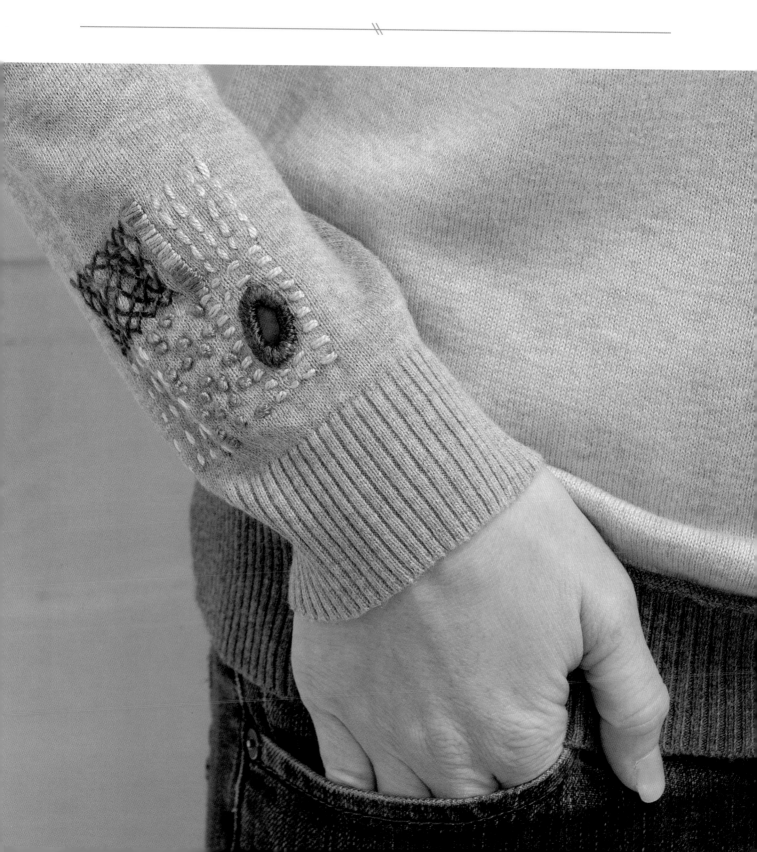

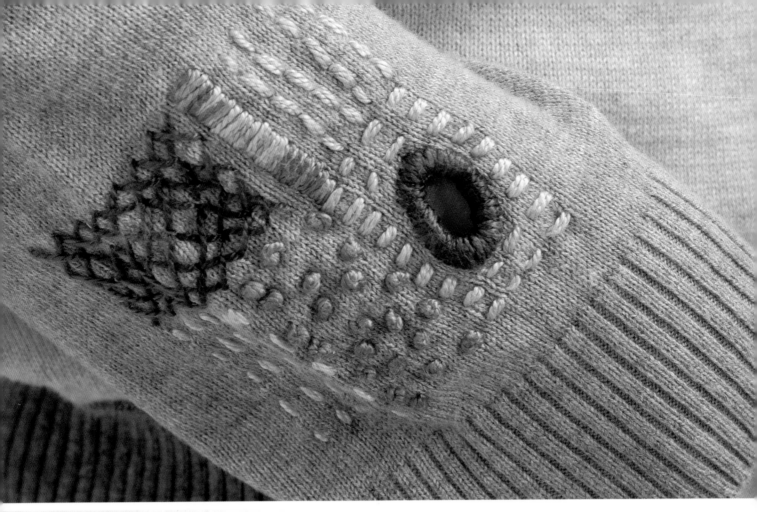

Women's Raglan-Sleeve Sweater

Once you've learned how to embroider several different stitches, why stop at mending just a hole? I turned the area surrounding the hole on this sweater sleeve into a little embroidery sampler. After backing the hole with a large square of wash-away stabilizer and sewing an eyelet stitch around the hole, I embellished around it using a grid layout, adding running stitches, satin stitches, cross-stitches, and French knots. I worked in five different shades of size 5 pearl cotton: three solid and two variegated colors.

Cassette-Tape T-Shirt

I love this old shirt—but for some reason I wore it while I was painting and peppered it with paint spatters. What was I thinking? To visibly mend the spatters, I stitched seed stitches around each one using two strands of floss in colors that matched the cassette tapes. I worked with a thin, fine-point embroidery needle, but when mending a knit fabric such as this one, you could also use a ballpoint or other blunt-tip hand-sewing needle. That will lessen the possibility of breaking additional knit threads as you sew.

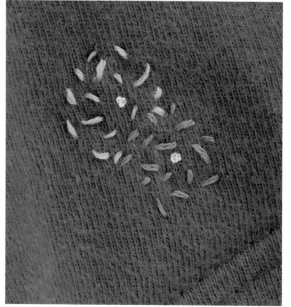

Linen Pants

Two growing holes in this pair of linen pants inspired me to plant a garden. I used single strands of size 5 pearl cotton in light green, dark green, yellow, light pink, dark pink, hot pink, sky blue, and violet. I started by wrapping holes in an eyelet stitch and then planned an embroidered garden around them. You can download and print the garden motif at ShopMartingale.com/VisibleMending or design your own! Enlarge or reduce the motif to fit your mendable area, print it out on wash-away stabilizer, and follow the stitches listed on the motif to complete your garden patch. I envisioned this as a colorful garden, but I think it would be fun to emulate the neutral shades of the linen as well.

Blue Miniskirt

Have you ever found a stain on an item and have no idea how it got there? That's what happened to this skirt. The stain looked like ink, but who knows? What was abundantly clear was that the stain was permanent. After backing the area with wash-away stabilizer, I embroidered around the stain using a satin stitch, following the irregular shape of the blot. Just for fun, I added French knots around the shape. If you're worried about your stitches coming undone over time or getting snagged, iron a square of permanent fusible interfacing to the wrong side of your work to cover and protect your stitching.

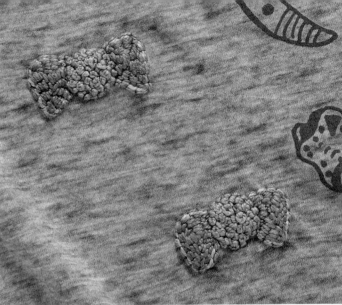

Elephant T-Shirt

The elephant motif drew me to this T-shirt; the holes scattered over the front made me love it even more because they gave me the perfect opportunity to get a little playful with my embroidery. Rather than just mend the holes, I decided to cover them with embroidered elephant heads and ears. First, I backed each hole with a small square of fusible interfacing (especially for knits), making sure the square extended far enough around the hole to accommodate the entire motif. On the front side, I used a penny as a template and a washable pen to draw a circle around each hole. Working with a fine-point embroidery needle and dark gray size 5 pearl cotton, I sewed closely spaced French knots on the circle and then spiraled in with my knots until I reached the center. (I don't use an embroidery hoop, but you may find it helpful for this type of embroidery). I then drew the ears, traced the motifs onto either side of each head, and outlined them in backstitching, first with dark gray pearl cotton and then with light gray pearl cotton. Finally, I filled in each ear with dark gray backstitches. You can draw the ears freehand or find them at ShopMartingale.com/VisibleMending.

Canvas Shoes

I have an embarrassingly large collection of canvas shoes. Over time, the rubber on the sides of the shoes can start to separate from the canvas. To keep the rubber and canvas from separating further on this pair, I repaired them with a satin stitch sewn with six strands of a pink variegated embroidery thread.

For easier sewing on a canvas shoe, remove the shoelace and pull the tongue toward the top of the shoe. Cut a piece of thread the length of your arm and thread a heavy-duty, sharp needle, such as a chenille needle. Poke the needle through the canvas on the inside of the shoe, about ⅛" from the rubber. Pull the needle to the outside, leaving a 6" tail (you'll weave this tail in when you're done stitching to avoid tying knots on the inside of the shoe).

Be sure to poke the rubber on the outside of the shoe and poke the canvas on the inside of the shoe—it's much easier to poke through the rubber when you can see from the outside where you need to poke. Because it can be hard to push and pull the needle through the rubber, use a thimble and pliers.

End your stitches on the inside of the shoe. Weave the beginning and end of the thread through the stitches on the inside of the shoe and cut the thread tails close to the stitching.

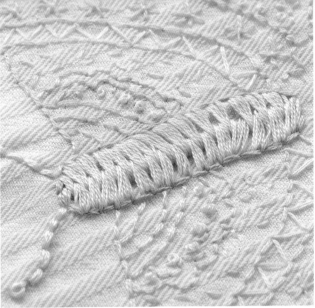

White Tablecloth

I inherited this white linen tablecloth from my grandmother, but it came with some spots that I couldn't get rid of. For a sweet, airy touch, I drew a butterfly motif, printed it out three times on wash-away stabilizer, and placed one over each spot. I embroidered the butterflies directly through the stabilizer in yellow, gray, and white using a variety of stitches and two strands of embroidery floss for two of the butterflies and a single strand of size 5 pearl cotton for the third. The stabilizer disappeared in a single washing. You can download and print this butterfly motif at ShopMartingale.com/VisibleMending. Enlarge or reduce it to fit your mend.

American Flag

For nearly 40 years, my dad flew this flag in front of our house every July. The flag had some L-shaped tears and other small holes that I wanted to repair, but I wanted the mends to be subtle and look the same from both sides of the flag (according to the American Legion, you can repair a flag as long as there's no distortion in the flag's shape or design). On the white stripes, I closed up the L-shaped tears with a satin stitch and worked additional rows of satin stitch to mend any small holes. For the mend on the red stripe, I created a satin-stitched square, drew a star in the center, and backstitched along the marked lines.

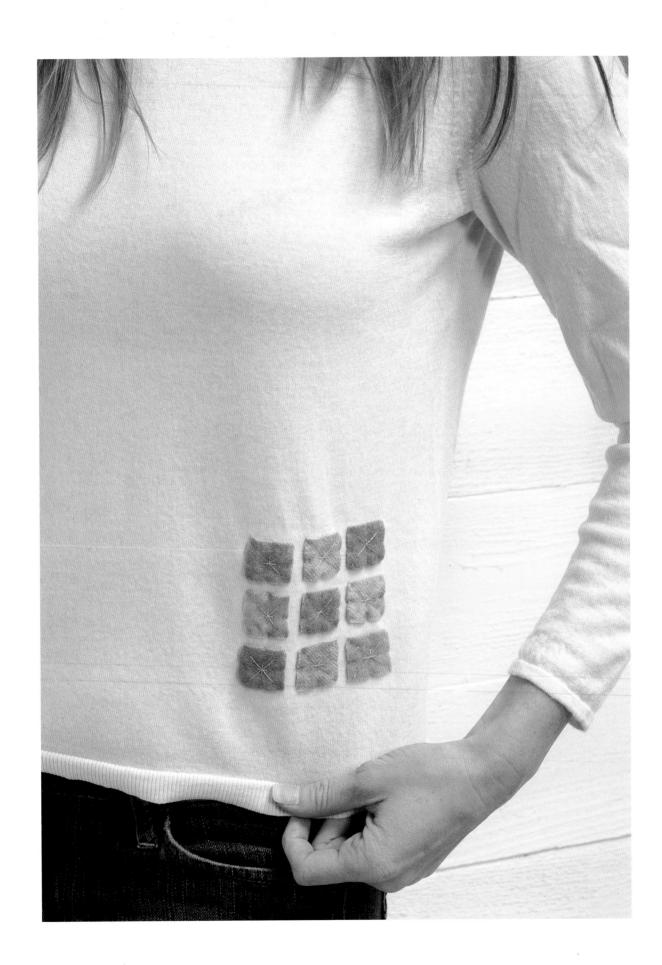

PATCHES

I know. It's a bit of a contradiction. Here you are, reading a book about visible mending, and you can plainly see that using patches to mend an item makes the area to be mended itself *in*visible! But patches can be the most visual kind of fix— and we're not talking about the stiff denim and corduroy patches you buy stapled to a piece of cardstock at the grocery store. None of that here. From hand-stitched patchwork to fussy-cut fabric motifs, patches are an easy way to mend and a fun way to get creative.

"Sewing mends the soul."

–Author unknown

MATERIALS FOR PATCHES

Here's what you'll need when working with patches.

Item in need of repair. Patches can cover most any kind of area to be mended, as long as the patch you've chosen is big enough to cover the damaged area and sturdy enough to keep it protected. Clothing, linens, blankets and quilts, upholstered furniture, and just about any other kind of textile item is patchable—if you're not sure how to mend something, it's patches to the rescue.

Patches. Patches can be made from all types of fabric and take just about any shape. A good general rule is to use a patch that's similar to your mendable item in weight and stretch. (But sometimes rules are made to be broken.)

Thread. Because the choices for applying patches are so varied, the threads you'll use to secure patches are varied as well—it all depends on your mendable item. I use common sewing thread to baste and appliqué patches by hand and machine, and embroidery thread and pearl cotton to embellish patches. Sometimes I use yarn in different weights to apply patches to heavier fabric, such as denim. Study your mendable area and make a plan; then choose a thread or yarn that best suits the fabric you'll be mending.

> *Thread Assessment*
>
> *If you're not sure what kind of thread will work best for a mendable area, look at the kind of thread that was originally used to create the item you're mending. Identifying the original thread may help you make a final decision.*

Hand-sewing needles. Because patches and thread can run the gamut in type and weight, which needle to use should be a thoughtful choice. As a general rule, choose the thinnest needle for the thread you're working with. I have a stash of needles at the ready: appliqué needles for common sewing thread, embroidery needles for embroidery thread, and heavier needles with large eyes (such as tapestry and darning needles) for thicker pearl cotton and yarn.

Wash-away stabilizer or fusible interfacing. Small holes, tears, and stains are easy to patch without stabilizer or interfacing, but larger holes need built-in stability before sewing. Even an extra-thin layer of featherweight stabilizer can increase stability as you stitch. Match the interfacing you're using to the fabric you're repairing—the manufacturer's instructions will clue you in about which interfacing to use for different fabrics. Be sure to use knit interfacing for knit fabric to keep the drape of the fabric similar to the rest of the item you're mending. For the greatest stability, cut interfacing to a size that overlaps a hole by at least ½" all around. See pages 9 and 10 for more information about stabilizers and interfacings.

Freezer paper. Freezer paper is a wonderful tool for creating curved appliqué shapes, such as circles. The freezer paper provides a firm edge to turn the raw edges of a patch to the back of the patch in preparation for hand appliqué. You'll find freezer paper at the grocery store among the foil and parchment papers, but I prefer to use Kim Diehl's Best Appliqué Freezer Paper produced by Martingale. It comes in 8½" × 11" sheets that lie flat, which makes for a much more pleasant experience than wrestling with the paper curling off the roll.

Sewing machine (optional). If you have a sewing machine, you can often make quicker work of patching items. I love to sew by hand, so that's usually my first choice—but when patching denim jeans (page 51), I often use a sewing machine to resew a seam that I've unpicked to set in a patch, giving the seam the same strength it had before I unpicked it. For patchwork-style patches, a sewing machine can be a time-saver too.

Hera marker (optional). A Hera marker is a tool with a wide, flat tip that helps you to mark and crease fabric. I use this tool to fold and crease raw edges of fabric to the back of a patch in preparation for hand appliqué. To temporarily crease the edge of a patch, use light to medium pressure as you drag the Hera marker (on dry fabric) or make small pressure dots (on damp fabric) along the fold.

Thimble, thread conditioner, glue stick, needle-nose pliers, and marking tools (optional). These items will make the process of applying patches easier. See pages 8 and 9 for a detailed explanation of each tool.

LEARNING TO SEW PATCHES

Appliqué is a go-to technique for sewing patches, but you might be surprised at how many ways there are to appliqué! Below are four of my favorite appliqué methods for applying patches. Or you can view a quick video introduction to each appliqué technique at ShopMartingale.com/VisibleMending.

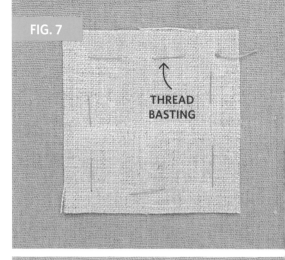

FIG. 7

THREAD BASTING

When in Doubt, Try It Out

Don't have a clear vision of how a mend will look in the end? Try your patch-and-thread theories on a practice piece first. Using a scrap of material similar to the item to be mended, create a sample patch with various thread choices to help you envision the result and streamline how to approach the task.

Raw-Edge Appliqué

1 Center a patch over the area to be mended, making sure the patch extends at least ½" beyond the hole or tear all around Glue or thread baste the patch in place (fig. 7).

2 With your choice of thread and a running stitch or backstitch, sew around the perimeter of the patch, ¼" from the edges (fig. 8). When working with cotton patches, you can machine wash and dry your project after mending to get a fluffy, frayed look.

FIG. 8

RUNNING STITCH

BACKSTITCH

Hand Appliqué

This technique works best with patches that have straight edges.

1 Lay a patch on an ironing board or pad, wrong side up. Spray one side of the patch with water; turn one edge of the fabric ¼" toward the wrong side of the fabric.

2 Use a Hera marker to make small pressure dots along the folded edge of the fabric to crease it; set the fold with an iron. Repeat on all sides of the patch (fig. 9).

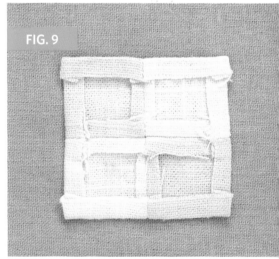

FIG. 9

3 Place the patch over the area to be mended. Thread baste; then whipstitch to appliqué the patch in place (fig. 10). Use your needle to push and tuck the raw edges of the patch underneath as you sew. If your patch has sharp corners (such as a square or triangle), take two whipstitches in place at each corner.

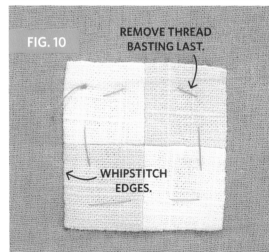

FIG. 10

REMOVE THREAD BASTING LAST.

WHIPSTITCH EDGES.

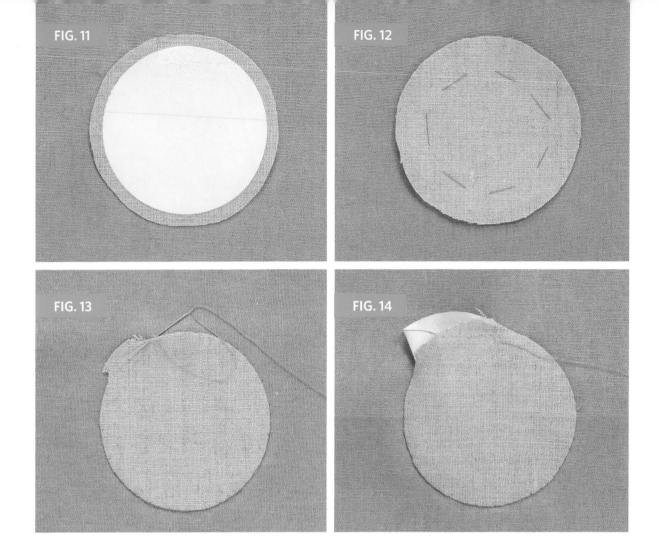

FIG. 11

FIG. 12

FIG. 13

FIG. 14

Freezer-Paper Appliqué

I find that this technique works best with patches that have curved edges.

1 On the dull side of the freezer paper, draw the shape of the patch you'll be using; cut out the shape on the drawn lines.

2 Iron the freezer paper, shiny side down, onto the wrong side of the patch fabric. Cut out the shape beyond the freezer paper by a scant ¼" (fig. 11).

3 Dot the freezer paper on the back of the patch with a glue stick; position the patch over the area to be mended and finger-press or thread baste in place (fig. 12).

4 Hand appliqué (page 41) the patch onto the item, using the needle to turn under the ¼" seam allowance as you go. Fold the raw edge of the patch tautly under the edge of the freezer paper, using your fingers to crease in place just beyond your stitching. Continue folding and stitching around the patch until you're approximately 10 to 20 stitches from the point where you started stitching (fig. 13).

5 With your fingers or with tweezers, gently tug at the freezer paper until it releases from the patch. Pull the freezer paper out of the seam opening (fig. 14). The freezer paper may tear into smaller pieces, which is fine—just make sure all of the freezer paper is removed. Fold under the remaining raw edge of the patch, finger-press to crease, and appliqué the opening closed.

English Paper Piecing

Dating back to the early 1700s, English paper piecing is a technique that is still alive and well—and it's fun! Here, hexagon-shaped paper templates are used as a guide to cut and sew fabrics together precisely.

1 Print out 2" and 1½" hexagon templates at ShopMartingale.com/VisibleMending; carefully cut out the templates on the drawn lines. Dot one side of a template with a glue stick and stick it to the wrong side of your mending fabric over the exact area of fabric that you want to show in your finished hexagon, such as the butterfly motif shown here. Cut the fabric a generous ¼" beyond the paper template (fig. 15).

2 Thread your needle with contrasting thread; knot the end. Fold one side's seam allowance to the back side of the template and baste long stitches through the fabric and paper. Baste the remaining five sides in the same way, making sure to capture each corner in your stitches; tie a knot flush with the fabric and clip the thread (fig. 16).

3 To join hexagons, thread a thin needle (such as an embroidery or appliqué needle) with thread that blends with the fabric; knot the end. Place the hexagons right sides together, matching the edges of the sides you're sewing together. Whipstitch small stitches along the edges of the hexagons, catching just two or three threads of the fabric on each side. Do not sew through the paper; only through the fabric. When you reach the end of one side, add additional hexagons in the same way. You may have to fold some pieces in half to line up and sew other pieces together (fig. 17).

4 When complete, press the piece on the back and front with an iron, remove the basting thread, and gently remove the paper pieces. Then use a whipstitch to appliqué the patch to your mendable item.

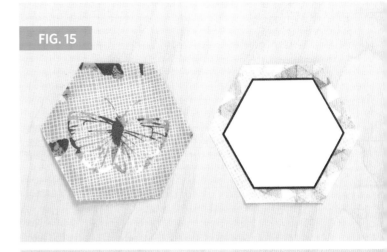

FIG. 15

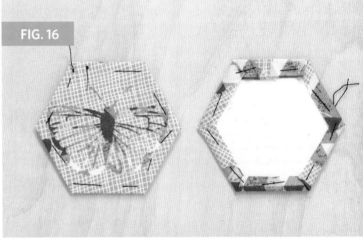

FIG. 16

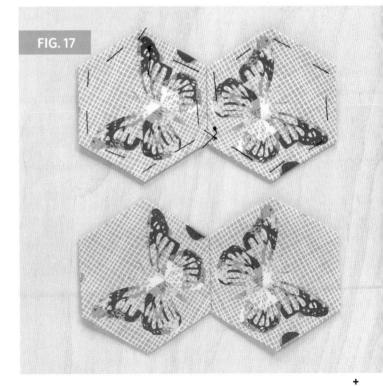

FIG. 17

PATCHES GALLERY

With basic appliqué skills, you can create oodles of different patches and sew them onto items in a variety of ways. Here are just a few examples of how patches can be used; consider them a jumping-off point to create your own patchy mends. For help with embroidery stitches, see page 23.

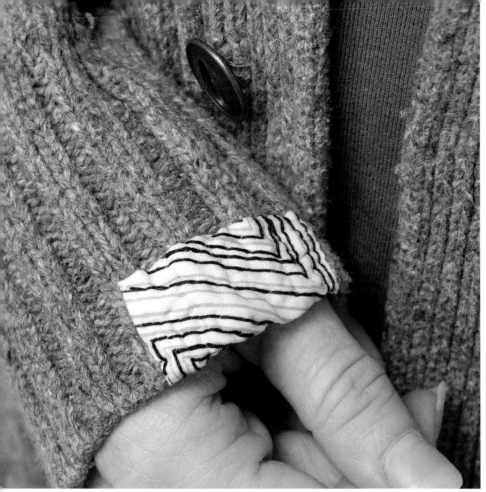

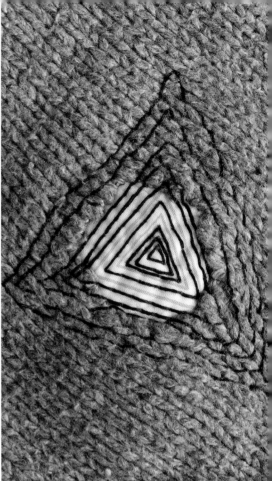

Boyfriend Cardigan

It's tempting to toss out a worn sweater, but repairing it is a fun challenge. I used the hand-appliqué technique to cover growing holes on both sleeves of this sweater and also mended some fraying at the cuff. I secured cotton-print patches over and under the worn areas using the lined patterns in the fabric as a stitch guide.

To make elbow mends a little cushier, sandwich a layer of quilt batting between two squares of fabric before appliquéing.

Prevent further unraveling of holes by backstitching around the perimeter, ¼" from the edges. Cut a patch at least ½" larger than the hole to be mended (for the hole shown at left, I fussy cut a triangle shape; see page 17). Use the hand-appliqué technique to secure the patch. If you like, use a backstitch to follow the patterns in the fabric for extra dimension.

To apply a patch that folds around an edge, as for a cuff, you'll need to cut the patch to extend beyond the area to be mended by at least ½" on all sides. Turn under the edges of the patch, press, and position so that half is on the outside of the cuff and half is folded around to the inner side of the cuff. Thread baste the patch in place, sewing through all three layers. Use the hand-appliqué technique to secure the patch to the cuff, again sewing through all three layers. If you like, use a backstitch to follow the patterns in your fabric to add dimension.

Girl's Dress

The Four Patch quilt-block design that covers what were several stains gives this dress additional personality. My large Four Patch starts with 1½" squares, and my small Four Patch with 1" squares. I used two contrasting colors of fabric for each Four Patch. If you need a larger mend, start with larger squares (in any color or colors), and keep in mind that when the design is sewn, the seam allowances will shrink your squares by ½".

Make the Four Patches by sewing the like-sized squares together using ¼" seam allowances. Then prepare the outer edges, referring to "Hand Appliqué" on page 41. Place the prepared patches over the stains and secure with hand appliqué stitches.

Bell-Bottom Denim

To successfully mend small holes, you probably don't need to apply interfacing. But if the drape of the fabric is distorted by a hole (or in the case of the featured jeans, several holes in the back of each pant leg), I generally cut a piece of fusible interfacing at least ½" larger than the hole all around, turn the pant leg wrong side out, and press the interfacing over the hole following the manufacturer's instructions.

For appliqué patches like these, make templates out of cardstock, trace around them onto the wrong side of the patch fabric, and then cut out the patches on the drawn lines. Use the raw-edge appliqué technique (page 41) to apply the patches.

For a decorative touch on leaf patches, work a stem stitch, adding an embroidered branch that weaves through the leaves and touches the base of each leaf. Finish with an embroidered midrib through the center of each leaf, again using the stem stitch.

Toddler Dress

There's no rule requiring stitchers to use the same technique to repair multiple holes in a single garment. In fact, mixing things up can be much more fun. I combined two appliqué techniques with fussy cutting to repair the two medium-sized holes in a toddler dress.

To make a similar repair, cut out a motif to use as a patch, adding a ¼" seam allowance all around. Use the freezer-paper appliqué technique to secure the motif to a patch of denim that has been cut larger than the motif by ¾" on all sides. Cut the denim patch so that it echoes the shape of the fussy-cut patch, keeping a ½" seam allowance all around. Center and sew the patch over the mendable area on your garment using a running stitch.

For embellishment, sew two rows of running stitches around the motif using variegated embroidery thread. Follow a few of the lines in the motif with a running stitch for added dimension.

Women's Wool Sweater

Since it isn't advisable to machine wash 100% merino wool, I saw this sweater as an opportunity to try a more delicate mend that could still endure hand washings. I covered a small hole with a quilt-block design in a Nine Patch style (bet you can't guess which patch the hole is under) using squares of hand-dyed, felted wool for the patches.

On the inside of the sweater, I applied a square of knit fusible interfacing that extends beyond the Nine Patch motif by ¼" on each side. For the embroidery on each patch, I used a single strand of metallic thread to take a whipstitch at each corner and at the center of each side, and then worked a star stitch in the middle.

Denim Hexie Jacket

After I caught this jacket on a wrought-iron chair, I used it as an opportunity to mend with English paper piecing. I sewed the hexagons together, appliquéd them to the jacket, and then embroidered around the outer edges and along each seam with pearl cotton and a backstitch. You can arrange hexagons in lots of different ways; play around with your hexagons to find an arrangement you like before sewing them together. Or patch mendable areas with a single hexagon, as I did on one of the jacket sleeves.

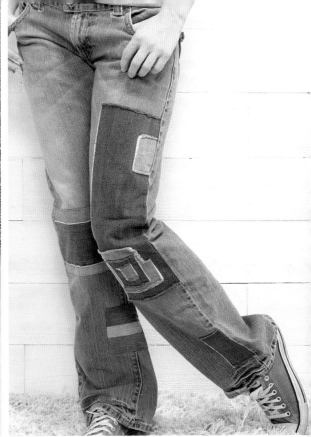

Light Denim

Like most of you, I have a favorite pair of jeans, and they have suffered more than a little wear and tear. To cover a significant area of weakening fibers in the left leg, I applied one big patch using raw-edge appliqué. Once I measured the size patch I needed, plus my ¼" seam allowance, I cut and appliquéd smaller patches to the big patch using the raw-edge appliqué technique. I finished with a machine stitch, but you could also use a running stitch or backstitch.

I unpicked the outer seam of the pant leg with a seam ripper, starting 1" above the hem and ending just above the area to be mended (there's no need to unpick the seam at the hem). I positioned my layered patch, making sure one edge of it was flush with the raw side seam I'd unpicked, and machine stitched the patch in place, again using raw-edge appliqué. I then added a second patch closer to the hem using the same technique. On this pant leg, I simply needed to turn it wrong side out and machine sew the unpicked seam back together.

Where I had worn a hole in the right leg at the knee as shown above right, I used a combination of hand appliqué and raw-edge appliqué by machine, turning the edges of the background patch under and leaving the edges of the layered patch raw. This repair required my unpicking both the inner and outer seams of the pant leg above the hem before applying the patch and stitching the inner side seam back in place. I added one more layered patch on top of that inner seam before sewing up the outer side seam. To mimic the gold stitch detail that I had unpicked, I sewed a backstitch down the inner seam of the pant leg in gold thread.

DARNING

Of all the visible-mending methods introduced, I think darning is the most challenging technique to learn. The good news is that once you understand the process, you might find that it's the most meditative of methods, and perhaps the most satisfying. Plus, you only need to have three things on hand: a needle, thread or yarn, and something to help stabilize the hole as you darn.

Darning is a lot like weaving. Instead of hiding a hole or sewing a hole closed, darning fills in a hole with woven thread or yarn, creating a new fabric in place of the fabric that's missing. The strength of a darning repair lies in the number of rows you sew over a hole, not how thick your thread or yarn is. Multiple narrow rows will result in the strongest mend.

"Repairing is caring."

–NudieJeans.com

MATERIALS FOR DARNING

Here's what you'll need when darning.

Item in need of repair. Darning is most practical for holes, rather than narrow tears or rips. Traditionally darning is used for repairing knit socks and sweaters, but I've experimented on different types of woven items, from linens to jeans. What I've found is that darning is useful for mending all sorts of woven items. The results are pretty, and the lattice weave with its standout texture offers design interest, even when you use thread or yarn in the same color as your mendable item.

Thread. Darning thread is one option, and it typically includes nylon, which adds strength. However, darning thread is hard to find, and the color choices are underwhelming. My general advice is to use a thread or yarn that is similar to your mendable item in both weight and fiber, but I don't always stick to that rule. I've tried cotton and wool yarn as well as pearl cotton and wool thread. I suggest experimenting with weights, fibers, and thicknesses of yarn and thread and choose what works best for your project. Sometimes combining different fibers is just the right thing—for example, I've darned holes in denim with a variegated wool sock yarn (page 61). Over several washes, the individual strands of wool begin to felt together, creating a fuzzy wool fabric all its own.

Hand-sewing needles. When you're using yarn to darn knits, darning needles are a must—they have a dull point at the tip, which stops the needle from breaking the knitted fabric fibers in the fabric, and their eyes are large enough for both thin and thick yarns. For woven items, I choose the thinnest needles possible with an eye that will accommodate the thickness of the thread or yarn I've chosen to work with.

Darning egg or mushroom. These tools are helpful for keeping the original contour and tension of an item while darning, especially with knits—not too tight, not too loose. I use a darning egg for more confined areas (think sleeves and socks) and a mushroom for places on a garment that are easier to reach (such as a hole on the front or back of a garment). The key is to place a darning egg or mushroom directly underneath a hole to hold the shape in place as you stitch and weave your thread or yarn. As a substitute, you could also use something similar in shape, such as a plastic Easter egg, the side of a cup or bowl, a baseball, a golf ball—even an apple, orange, or lemon will do the trick, if you don't poke into the fruit with your needle!

Wash-away stabilizer (for darning woven fabric). When darning woven items, I use a patch of wash-away stabilizer in addition to a darning egg or mushroom; it does the same job, keeping the original shape of a hole intact as I stitch. Another alternative is to back a hole on a woven item with netting, such as tulle. Simply thread baste a patch of netting on the wrong side of a hole before darning to retain the hole's original shape, darn the item, and remove the basting stitches. The stabilizer washes away, while the tulle is permanent.

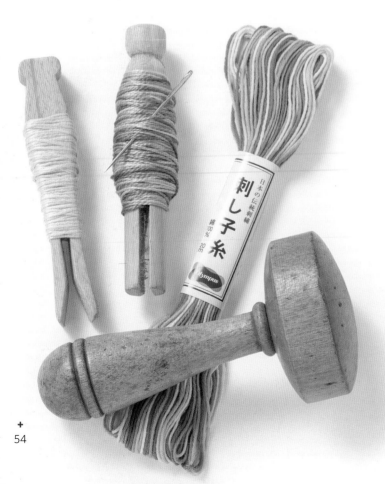

LEARNING TO DARN

There are three basic steps to darning: stitch around the hole (for nonwovens such as stretchy knits and sweater knits) or stabilize the hole (for cotton, linen, and other woven fabric); stitch across the hole; and finally, weave over and under the previous stitching. When you stitch across the hole, you'll create long stitches that jump from one side of the hole to the other side. When you weave, you'll work in a direction perpendicular to the long stitches, carrying your thread or yarn in and out of the rows of stitching. Some people like to darn from the wrong side, but that's to lessen the visibility of the mend. For a visibly mended look, darn from the right side. To view a quick video introduction on darning, visit ShopMartingale.com/VisibleMending.

Darning Stretchy Knits and Sweater Knits

1 Thread your needle with a long strand of your chosen yarn or thread (I use a strand that's at least 1½ times the length of my arm.

2 Begin by backstitching about ¼" from the edge of a hole, sewing around the "healthy" parts of the hole—the parts that are intact and not damaged (fig. 18). Backstitching does two things: First, it provides tension that preserves the original shape of the hole so it won't stretch while you're darning. Second, it gives you a path to follow as you sew long stitches over the hole.

3 Once your backstitching is complete, place a darning egg or mushroom or other slightly rounded item underneath the hole (fig. 19). This helps further preserve the shape of the garment, particularly where a hole is in an area that requires extra stretch (an elbow, a heel, and so on.)

4 Working from the wrong side of your piece, insert your needle next to a backstitch on the side that's farthest away from the hole; pull your thread or yarn through to the right side. Carry your stitch to the other side of the hole and insert your needle on the side of the backstitching that's farthest away from the hole. Pull the thread or yarn through, making the long stitch taut against the darning egg or mushroom but not so tight or loose that it distorts the original shape of the hole (fig. 20).

5 Keep turning your work and continue to sew closely spaced rows of running stitches and long stitches that carry over the hole. When you've covered the hole with long stitches and reached the other side, sew at least two rows of running stitches to anchor your stitches to the healthy part of the item.

6 Turn your work 90° and begin weaving your thread or yarn over and then under each long strand. Stitch and weave each vertical row until you've reached the other end of the hole. When you're satisfied with your weave, anchor your darning to the healthy part of the item with at least two more rows of running stitches (fig. 21).

7 Weave in the beginning and end of your thread or yarn on the wrong side of your work.

For items made of thicker yarn or thread, like this sweater, space the horizontal rows farther apart. For items made of thinner yarn or thread and for woven items, sew the rows closer together.

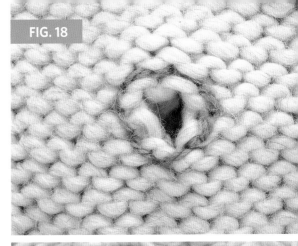

FIG. 18

FIG. 19

FIG. 20

FIG. 21

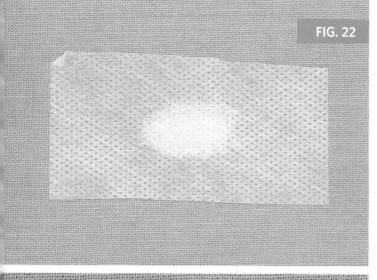

FIG. 22

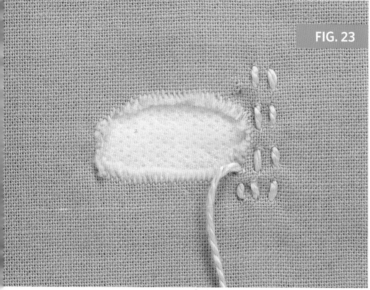

FIG. 23

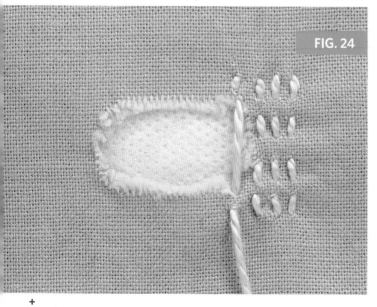

FIG. 24

Darning Cotton, Linen, and Other Woven Fabric

1 If darning woven fabric, do not backstitch; instead, back the mendable area with wash-away stabilizer to hold the fibers in place for darning (fig. 22).

2 Thread your needle with a long strand of your chosen yarn or thread. (As with knits, I like to use a strand that is at least 1½ times the length of my arm to ensure I'll get from the beginning to the end of my darning without needing a second strand.)

3 Anchor your stitches to the right of the hole by sewing two to three rows of running stitches on the healthy part of the fabric, stopping approximately ¼" from the bottom of the hole (make sure you're still inside the "healthy" part of the fabric). You can sew more rows in this healthy area, but be sure to sew a minimum of two rows. It's important to anchor your stitches to the healthy part of the item so your darning stitches have a sturdy foundation for long-term support (fig. 23).

4 Insert your needle from the wrong side of your work and pull your thread or yarn through to the right side. Carry your needle to the top of the hole and insert it ¼" (or less) beyond the hole, making sure you catch the healthy part of the fabric. Pull the thread or yarn through to make the long stitch taut but not so tight or loose that it distorts the original shape of the hole (fig. 24).

FIG. 25

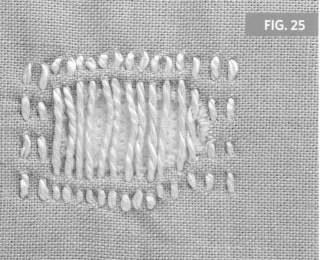

FIG. 26

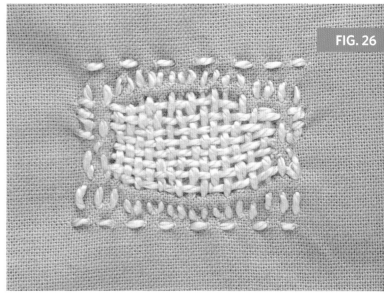

5 Turn your work and sew in the opposite direction the same way, ⅛" from your first row of stitches. Keep turning your work and continue to sew closely spaced rows of running stitches and long stitches that carry over the hole. When you've covered the hole with long stitches and reached the other side of the hole, sew at least two rows of running stitches to anchor your stitches to the healthy part of the item (fig. 25).

6 Turn your work 90°. Sew at least one row of running stitches horizontally across the healthy part of the item. When you reach the long vertical stitches over the hole, weave your thread or yarn over and then under each long strand. Stitch and weave each horizontal row until you've reached the other end of the hole. When you're satisfied with your weave, anchor your darning to the healthy part of the item with at least one more row of running stitches (fig. 26).

7 Weave in the beginning and end of your strand on the wrong side of your work.

I surrounded these darned areas with three rows of backstitching; see page 61 for the how-to.

DARNING GALLERY

Finished darning can appear bold and chunky or refined and delicate, depending on the item you're mending and the thread or yarn you use. Here are a few ways I've used darning in my visible mends. For help with embroidery stitches, see page 23.

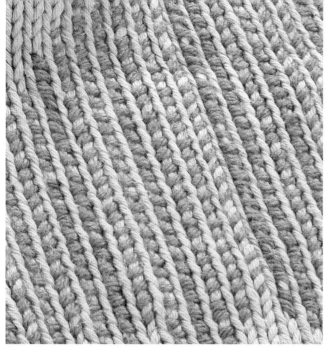

Cardigan Sweater

The holes in the elbow and at the neckline of this cardigan were the perfect candidates for darning. When I finished the elbow, the resulting visible darn had a shape that reminded me of a cat—and that wasn't what I was going for! So I decided to whipstitch a rectangular box around the darning, using the loops and ladders of the knitted fabric as a guide. I kept adding rows of whipstitching in different lengths—I couldn't seem to stop—and ended up sewing whipstitched rows around the entire sleeve, until the rows met the other side of the darning.

Blue Button-Up Shirt

I admit, this was an experiment—I wasn't sure pulling fabric strips through a woven fabric would work, especially with an existing hole in the elbow.

It did require a bit of gentle tugging, but I'm happy with the result (and more importantly, my husband is happy—it's his shirt, after all!). I cut ¼"-wide strips no more than 16" long from two different blue prints and wove one fabric horizontally and the other fabric vertically. I knew that the blue strips would fray as I pulled them in and out of the fabric, but I liked how that amplified the texture. I think this technique would work equally well on sweaters, and it wouldn't require as much tugging.

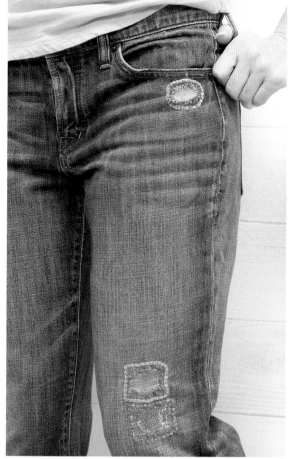

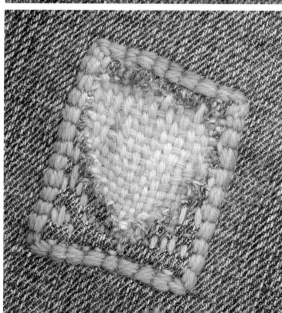

Boyfriend Jeans

I darned multiple holes in these jeans with variegated wool sock yarn, which changed colors from hole to hole. Holding the original shape of the holes in place with patches of wash-away stabilizer, I simply stitched and weaved. After darning, I fused patches of medium-weight fusible interfacing on the back of each hole for added strength and stability, and then framed each darned hole with backstitches for additional embellishment.

I kept the weaving in place so you could clearly see the darning, but over time these jeans will be washed and dried (on a short and gentle cycle) and the wool yarn will felt together, making a new wool fabric to cover the holes.

Striped Wool Hat

The tiny hole beginning to form on this wool hat took just a few minutes to darn. I chose a red yarn that mimicked the red in the hat but contrasted with the area to be darned. I also backstitched a little star on the brim in red yarn for a bit of added fun.

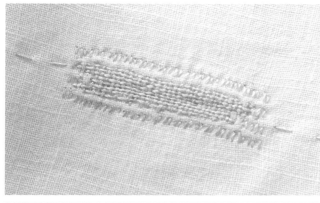

Antique Tablecloth

My sister gave me this tablecloth, which was previously owned by my grandma. It came with a few small holes and a stain that I wasn't able to wash away. I darned the holes with an Aurifil 12-weight silvery thread (the color is called Light Robin's Egg). I embroidered a ¼"-wide satin stitch around the perimeter of the stain to enhance it, rather than disguise it. When my visible mending was complete, I noticed that the four places I mended were somewhere in the vicinity of the four corners of the tablecloth itself. So for added embellishment, I used a running stitch to sew a winding, curvy line that touched each of the four mended areas.

MENDING BY MACHINE

As much as I love mending by hand, mending by machine brings a lively pace and its own brand of fun—at 100 miles an hour! With a simple straight stitch, you can angle, curve, and seesaw your way around mendable areas, with patches or without. And with a free-motion foot—typically used for machine quilting—you can really go wild with your stitching. It's so easy to get hooked on these techniques, you'll be grabbing a seam ripper to make a tear or hole, just for the fun of mending the machine way.

> *"The most sustainable shirt in the world is the one that already exists."*
>
> –Value Village

MATERIALS FOR MACHINE MENDING

Here's what you'll need when mending by machine.

Item in need of repair. Machine mending works best with woven fabric, such as denim and cotton, but with ballpoint machine needles you can also mend knits. The only time I might not use machine mending is if an item is extremely delicate, where a sewing machine may do more harm than good.

Patches. Just like in the patches chapter, coverings for holes can run the gamut—most any fabric, most any shape—and they can sit in front of or behind a mendable area. A good general rule is to use a patch that's similar to your mendable item in weight and stretch—but break the rules if that's where your creativity leads you.

Thread. The types of machine-sewing threads available seem virtually endless. Online charts cover details about thread weight and usage, and just about every thread manufacturer has one. What's important to note is that the higher the thread number, the thinner the thread. For machine mending, I prefer a #40 or a #50 weight thread. (If you see a number such as #50/2 or #50/3, the second number refers to the ply; the more plies in the thread, the stronger the thread.) I use both cotton and polyester thread, which is available in a rainbow of colors at your local fabric shop and online.

Sewing machine. For the techniques in this chapter, you'll need a machine in good working order that can sew a straight stitch and a zigzag stitch, and you'll also need a free-motion foot (available at sewing-machine dealer stores and online; look in your machine's manual to make sure you get a foot that works with your machine). If your sewing machine has the capability to do decorative stitches, experiment with them—you may find some that work beautifully for sewing, embellishing, and mending all at the same time.

Machine-sewing needles. I keep a stash of three types of needles: universal needles (size 90/14, for woven fabric); ballpoint needles (90/14, for knit fabric); and denim needles (100/16, for denim and other heavy fabric). Switch needles depending on the fabric you're sewing.

Wash-away stabilizer. When mending by machine, I stick a square of wash-away stabilizer on the wrong side of almost every mendable item. Machines go fast—without stabilizer, you can accidentally "shrink" holes and tears and wind up with puckers. The stabilizer provides temporary support and preserves the original shape of the area while you sew by machine. Plus, it washes away with water. The only time I don't use stabilizer is when I'm applying a heavy fabric patch, such as denim, which holds the shape of a hole or tear just fine by itself.

Scissors, glue stick, rotary equipment. These items will make the process of mending by machine easier. See pages 8 and 9 for details.

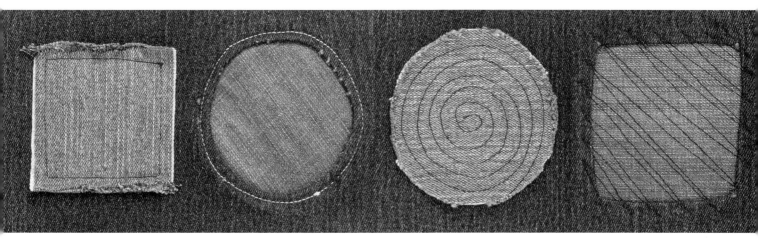

From left to right: traditional square patch with raw edges and straight stitches; reverse-appliqué circle with turned-under edges and straight stitches; traditional circle patch with raw edges and straight-stitch design; reverse-appliqué square with turned-under edges and straight-stitch design

LEARNING TO MEND BY MACHINE

In contrast to the other mending techniques, machine sewing is fast-paced and the mends are typically quicker to finish. Below are three ways to mend by machine. To view a quick video introduction to mending by machine, visit ShopMartingale.com/VisibleMending.

Mending by Machine with Straight Stitches and Patches

A straight stitch doesn't mean you must only sew in a straight line—there's fun to be had with angles and curves too.

1 Cut a piece of wash-away stabilizer big enough to cover your mendable area by at least ½" on all sides; smooth out the item to be mended on a flat surface and stick the stabilizer to the wrong side of your mendable area.

2 Cut a patch to the same size as the wash-away stabilizer. For a traditional patch on top of a mendable area, dot the wrong side of the patch with a glue stick and press it in place to cover the spot. For a patch behind your mendable area, glue the front of the patch and press it in place right side out on the back of your item. You can leave a hole's edges raw and allow them to fray, or you can fold, press, and glue the raw edges of a hole to the wrong side by ¼" for a more finished look. The technique of applying your patch from behind to a shaped opening is generally referred to as reverse appliqué. If the hole has sharp corners to turn, such as a square, clip diagonally into each corner a scant ¼"; for curves, such as a circle, clip into the curve a scant ¼" every ¼". Clipping makes the edges easier to fold, press, and glue under to the wrong side.

3 A machine straight stitch lets you secure patches in a variety of ways (the default stitch length on my machine is 2.5, and that's what I typically use). Sometimes I simply sew around the perimeter of a patch, and in other situations I sew on top of and beyond the patch. In all cases, be sure to extend your patch, and thereby your stitches, beyond a hole or tear by at least ½" all around.

Free-Motion Machine Mending

No patches are needed with free-motion work; instead, the thread you sew with becomes your patch. If you've never sewn with a free-motion sewing-machine foot, practice the technique to get a feel for the back-and-forth motion before trying it on an actual mend. This is the technique I use to mend with free-motion stitching:

1 Install a free-motion foot on your machine. Drop the feed dogs on your machine or leave them up—it's really a personal preference, so try it both ways on a fabric scrap to determine what you like best. Leaving the feed dogs up provides a little more grip while free-motion sewing.

2 Cut a square of wash-away stabilizer big enough to cover a hole or rip by at least ½" all around; smooth out the mendable spot on a flat surface and stick the stabilizer to the wrong side.

3 Position the mendable area under the needle so the needle is about ½" above the

mendable area and about ½" to one side of it. Make two to three stitches on top of each other to lock the thread in place.

4 Sew with a back-and-forth motion, guiding the fabric toward you and then away from you, angling your stitches as you sew, so they make pointy peaks across the mendable area. Sew across the entire width of the area, making sure your stitches extend at least ½" past the area all around.

5 Once you reach one edge of the area you're mending, start stitching in the opposite direction. Sew across the area as many times as you like; I take at least three or four passes. Make two to three stitches on top of each other to lock the thread in place. Remove the item from the machine and clip all thread close to the fabric.

6 Optional: Turn your item 90° and repeat steps 2 and 3 to finish the mend.

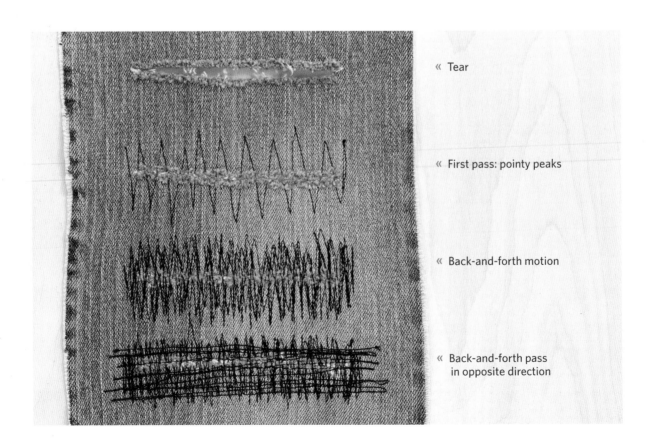

« Tear

« First pass: pointy peaks

« Back-and-forth motion

« Back-and-forth pass
   in opposite direction

Free-Motion Machine Mending with Patches

Apply your patch in front of a mendable area (traditional patch) or behind it (reverse appliqué); the look is up to you, and the technique is essentially the same for both kinds of mends. Both work well for strengthening larger holes and tears.

1 Cut a patch big enough to cover the hole or tear by ½" all around. For a traditional patch, dot the wrong side of the patch with a glue stick, and press it in place to cover your mendable area. For a reverse-appliqué patch, glue the front of the patch and press it in place, right side out, on the back of your item. (In either case, if you're working with stretchy fabrics, such as a cotton or sweater knit, add a patch of wash-away stabilizer before applying your patch to preserve the shape of the hole before sewing.) If you like, also thread baste the patch to the item for additional stability; remember to remove the basting thread when you've completed your stitching.

2 Follow steps 2–4 in "Free-Motion Machine Mending" (page 68) to secure a patch to a hole, or experiment a little more with free-motion stitching. In my examples, I free-motion stitched around the first hole in a circular motion. For the second hole, I also free-motion stitched but with a back-and-forth motion around the hole, creating a sunburst effect (figs. 27 and 28).

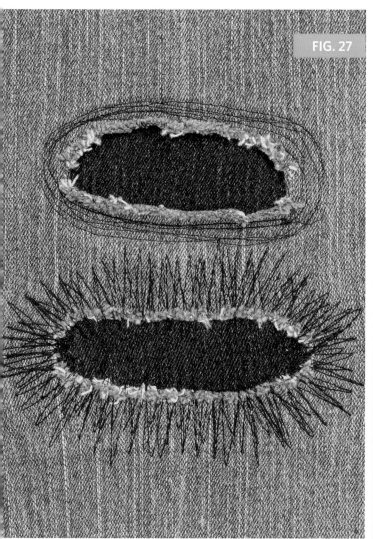

FIG. 27

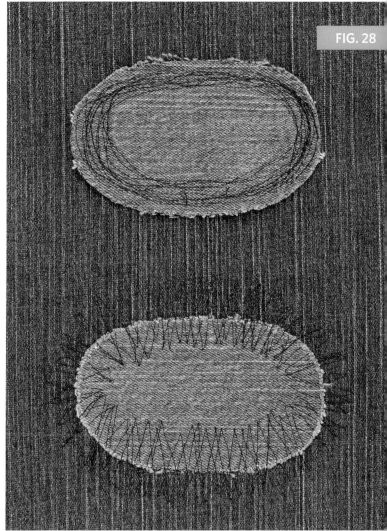

FIG. 28

MACHINE-MENDING GALLERY

You and your trusty machine can get so creative with mending! My wardrobe of machine-mended items is ever growing. Each time I repair a well-loved piece, I feel as if I've created a one-of-a-kind garment to love all over again.

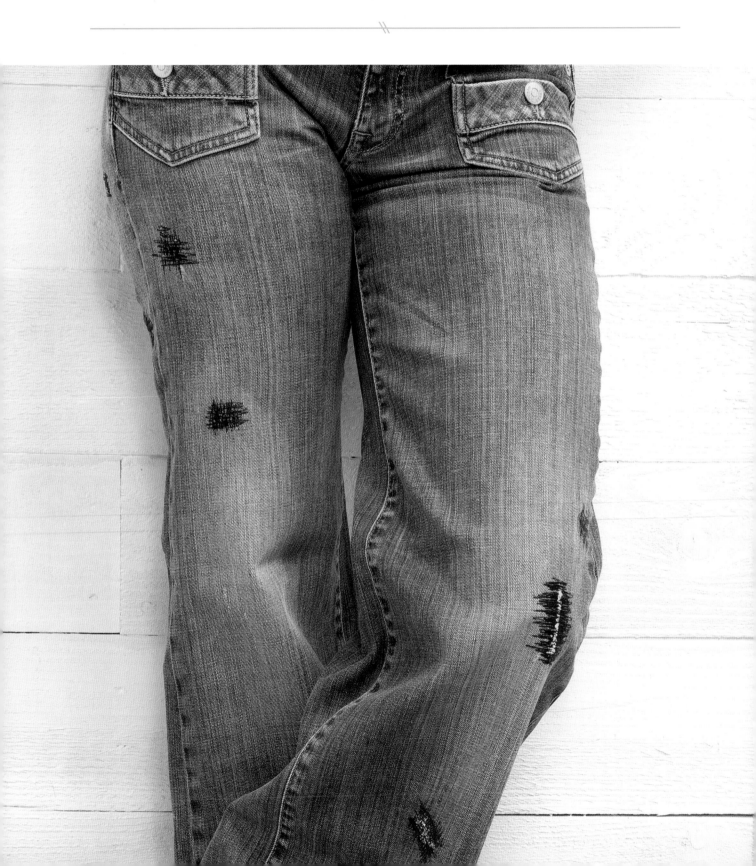

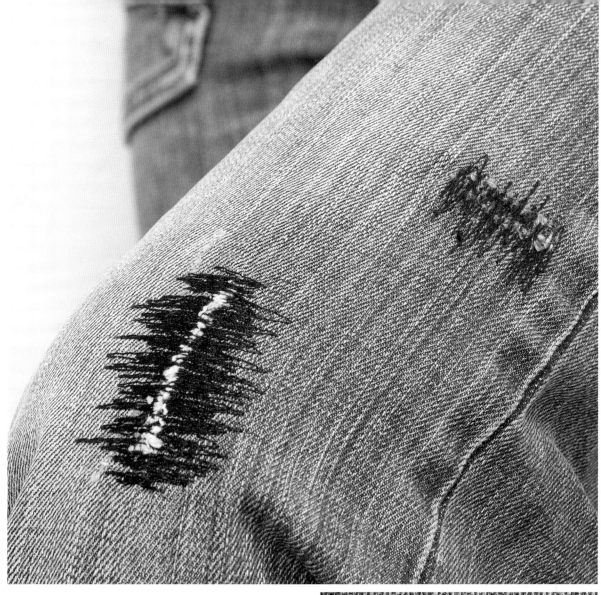

Denim Jeans (Small Holes)

You know how your jeans start to get those little threadbare areas as you wash, dry, and wear them over time? On this pair, I used free-motion mending to repair several spots where holes were about to start. Just as with the patched jeans on page 51, I unpicked the outer seam of the pant leg with a seam ripper, starting 1" above the hem and ending 1" to 2" above the areas to be mended. When my machine mending was complete, I machine sewed the unpicked seam back together. Free-motion mending is not only one of my favorite ways to repair small holes and tears—it's one of the quickest!

Denim Jeans (Large Holes)

Ah, the knee mend! A knee repair must be strong, and you want it to last. For this mend—or any other where you're addressing curves, such as elbows and crotches—machine stitching with a patch is the way to go. In the case of these jeans, the knee holes were both horizontal and vertical. Just as with the patched jeans on page 51, I used a seam ripper to unpick the outer seam of each pant leg, starting 1" above the pant cuff and ending 1" to 2" above the areas to be mended. I left the edges of the holes raw, and secured the denim patches to each knee by free-motion stitching around the natural shape of the holes. When my machine mending was complete, I machine sewed the unpicked seam back together.

Striped Jacket

Directional fabric can really add fun to your mending. Two holes had already started forming in this jacket, so I simply made them bigger, giving myself a reason to create a more visible mend. For my circle template, I used a spice-container lid, centering it over each hole and tracing around it using an air-soluble marker. I used the reverse-appliqué technique, turning under the edges of the holes for a finished edge. For my patches, I cut circles out of a darker striped fabric, approximately ½" larger than my circle template. Working from the wrong side of the jacket, I glued and centered my patches over the prepared holes, right side out, and then straight stitched around the holes from the right side of the jacket with a ⅛" seam allowance. Depending on the patch fabric you use, you can match up stripes or turn them perpendicularly or diagonally for different effects.

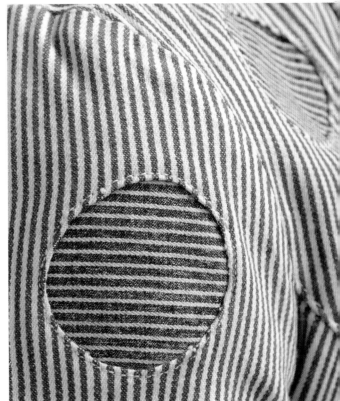

Black Button-Up Shirt

Two small holes developing in the shoulder of this button-up shirt inspired a functional patch mend that quickly conceals the damage. I cut seven 1½" cotton squares in black and shades of gray and then cut each square in half diagonally. I glued triangle pairs right sides together and then glued the doubled triangles to the shirt in two horizontal rows, making sure to adequately cover the mendable areas. Using an air-soluble marker and a ruler, I drew diagonal guidelines across the triangle shapes, ¼" apart, and machine sewed over the lines using a straight stitch. When the shirt was machine washed and dried, the triangle edges frayed and gave the mend a more dimensional look.

Striped Sweater

I often turn to my stash of cutter sweaters for interesting sweater mends. A cutter sweater is simply a sweater that's used for harvesting patches; sweaters you don't wear anymore, thrifted sweaters, or old sweaters that family and friends are ready to retire will work. Tightly knit sweaters work best for patches (avoid loosely knit, lacy sweaters). Because cutter-sweater patches will unravel and stretch, it's important to prepare them properly.

I repaired the damage at the elbow of a striped sweater and tossed on a little decorative cutter patch by first applying a piece of wash-away stabilizer to the inside of the cutter sweater, large enough to cover the area to be patched. After cutting out the patch along the edges of the stabilizer, I finished the edges of the patch by zigzag stitching around it. I thread basted the patch over the damaged area and secured the patch to the sweater with several rows of straight stitching across the patch, spaced ¼" apart.

For extra embellishment, I added a smaller patch to the body of the sweater, even though there was no hole to be covered.

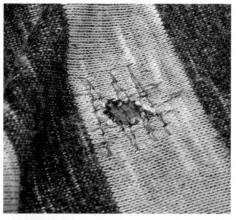

Striped Knit T-Shirt

I frequently use this machine technique for mending little holes that start to form in knit fabric. I backed each hole with a square of wash-away stabilizer that I cut ½" larger than each hole on all sides. I then cut a square of knit fabric—in this case, teal knit—to the same size as the stabilizer square and glued it, right side out, to the stabilizer. (On the front of the item, you'll see the stabilizer, not the knit fabric, showing through the hole. That's OK, because the stabilizer will wash away). Using a ballpoint machine needle and a straight stitch, I sewed pointy peaks (think about drawing the letter *V* with your needle) across each hole both vertically and horizontally to secure the patches in place. After washing and drying the shirt to dissolve the stabilizer, I turned the shirt right side out and clipped the teal square ⅛" from the machine stitching.

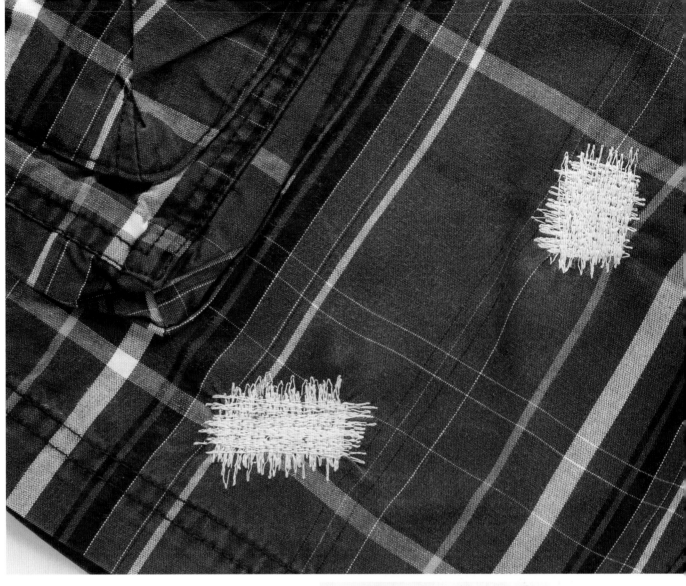

Boy's Shorts

I addressed two small holes in these shorts with free-motion stitching—no patches needed! I applied squares of wash-away stabilizer to the back of the holes to stabilize them and maintain the lines of the plaid as I sewed angled lines (in free-motion) across the holes, both horizontally and vertically. The threads stitched within the holes interlocked, forming their own fabric, while the stitches sewn beyond the perimeter of the holes anchored the newly formed fabric to the garment.

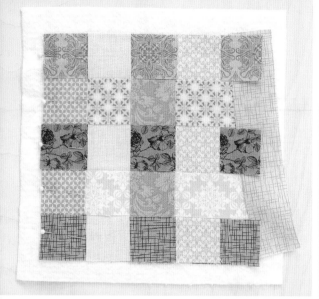

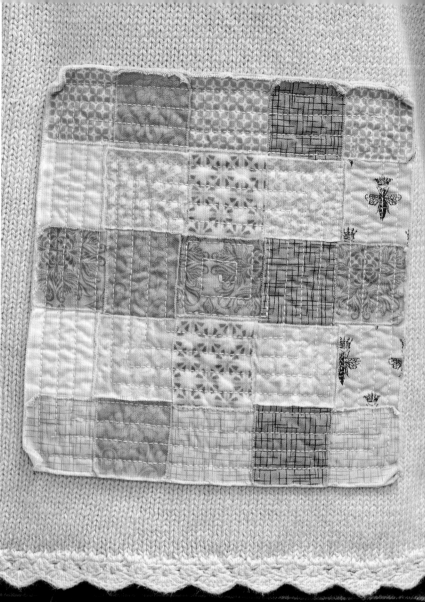

Crocheted Sweater

An unraveling hole on the back of this sweater inspired a big visible mend, and I used a woven quilt block as my patch. To prepare the sweater, I cut away the loose thread around the hole, and with doubled sewing thread I backstitched by hand around the hole to prevent further unraveling. The backstitching also helped set the shape of the sweater, making it easier for me to apply my patch.

Before applying my woven patch, I positioned a piece of wash-away stabilizer over the hole on the right side of the sweater, finger-pressing it in place. Because the patch was so large, I basted it in place with both glue and thread to further minimize shifting during sewing. To secure the patch, I stitched a square spiral from the edges toward the center, spacing the stitching lines ¼" apart. As for the patch edges, I left those raw (rather than turning them under) so that they'd get soft and fluffy after laundering.

RESOURCES

Many thanks to these companies for providing
me with quality fabric, thread, and notions.

SULKY OF AMERICA
Sulky.com

MODA FABRICS
UnitedNotions.com

ART GALLERY FABRICS
ArtGalleryFabrics.com

AURIFIL
Aurifil.com

DMC
DMC-USA.com

CLOVER NEEDLECRAFT, INC.
Clover-USA.com

PELLON
Stick-N-Washaway stabilizer
PellonProjects.com

THE WARM COMPANY
Steam-A-Seam 2 double-stick fusible web
WarmCompany.com

ACKNOWLEDGMENTS

To Brett, Jack, and Charlie: thank you for supporting me as my idea-bouncers, my cheerleaders—
and sometimes even my models!—throughout the creation of this book. I love you.

To the mighty team at Martingale: thank you for once again taking a chance on me. I've worked
at Martingale for more than 15 years now, and I still come to work excited to see what's next. The
people at this one-of-a-kind company make my job a joy. A special thanks to Publisher and Chief
Visionary Officer Jennifer Keltner, who spotted the makings of a book from my inkling of an idea.

ABOUT THE AUTHOR

Follow Jenny online:

RemadeNation.com

Instagram: @visible.mending

Jenny Wilding Cardon has been creating with fabric since high school. Back then, she would design eccentric, rebellious items of clothing, and then make her friends wear them to school. After graduating from college in Utah with a degree in Women's Studies, Jenny spent three years with her husband in Seattle, where she quickly caught the quilting bug from her coworkers at Martingale.

Jenny worked as a copywriter for Martingale one day short of 10 years before giving up her position to be a stay-at-home mom. In 2011, she returned to Martingale as their content editor, and now spends most of her work time writing for Martingale's Stitch This! blog.

The birth of her first son inspired Jenny to write her first pattern collection, *The Little Box of Baby Quilts* (Martingale, 2007). Her second, the book *ReSew* (Martingale, 2011), paired her two creative outlets—thrifting and sewing. Jenny's designs have also appeared on the covers of *Quilts and More* and *Quilt It for Kids* magazines, as well as in *McCall's Quilting* and *Simple Quilts and Sewing*.

Jenny lives on an acre in a Utah farming town with her husband of 18 years and their two sons, Jack and Charlie. Since the commute to the Martingale office is 818.64 miles, the bosses typically allow her to work from home.

31901064006630